TRUTH PLUS LOVE

STUDY GUIDE | SIX SESSIONS

THE *JESUS* WAY TO INFLUENCE

MATT BROWN

WITH DUDLEY DELFFS

ZONDERVAN®

Truth Plus Love Study Guide
© 2019 by Matt Brown

Requests for information should be addressed to: *Zondervan, 3900 Sparks Dr. SE, Grand Rapids, Michigan 49546.*

ISBN 978-0-310-11233-4 (softcover)
ISBN 978-0-310-11234-1 (ebook)

First Printing June 2019 / Printed in the United States of America

CONTENTS

INTRODUCTION

Christians today are facing a crisis of influence. So many people dismiss us as either being too rigid and judgmental in our convictions or too soft and easygoing in our response to challenging and complex issues. And with social media as our megaphone, we can now comment on *anything* and *everything*—often without thinking through how it might come across to others . . . especially to those whose only knowledge of God comes from us.

It's one thing to stand up for our convictions. But if we're only adding static to the cultural conversation, we're not communicating the essence of the gospel. Similarly, we can "like" and "friend" as many people as we want, but if we are not boldly sharing the reality of who Christ is and what he did for each of us, we are also not likely to have an impact on others.

What we need is a better, more balanced way. We need to communicate the *truth* of our sinful condition by employing the grace and *love* of God. We see Jesus displaying this exact balance throughout his ministry on earth. He always relied on the foundation of God's Word as the source of his truth even as he showed loving compassion to everyone in need—the sick, the hurting, the lonely, the grieving, and the guilty alike. He met their needs in order to uncover the deeper spiritual hunger that only his love could fill.

As followers of Jesus, we are called to show others *truth plus love*. The Bible talks a lot about getting this balance right. In the first half of Paul's letter to the Ephesians, he issued no direct commands to his readers other than to "remember" . . . which means he didn't tell them to "do" anything new. He simply called them back to the gospel—the main event of history itself—and encouraged them to be captivated by all God had done for them.

But in the second half of the letter, Paul issued *forty* direct commands to his readers. In effect, he was telling them what they should now do based on the truth of the gospel they had come to believe. One of these powerful commands is found in Ephesians 4:15, where Paul writes, "Speaking the *truth in love*, we are to grow up in every way into him who is the head, into Christ" (ESV, emphasis added).

There it is—truth plus love—the formula for influencing our world. And if we do this, the promise is we will "grow up in every way" in Jesus Christ. Unfortunately, as you likely have come to understand, it's tough to get this balance right. But that is what this study is about. In the sessions that follow, I want to help you strike this balance between truth and love as you produce the spiritual fruit that Paul outlines in Galatians 5:22–23: *love, joy, peace, patience, kindness, goodness, faithfulness, gentleness,* and *self-control.*

As you practice the habits that yield this kind of spiritual fruit, it is my belief you will grow in your relationship with Christ and be a follower who gets the balance right . . . a life of standing for the *truth* of God while demonstrating the *love* of God. It's my prayer that the lessons I share, and the wisdom I've received from the Bible as I've walked through trials, will serve to flood your own heart with comfort, wisdom, and power from God.

So, are you ready for the journey? Let's jump in and begin.

—Matt Brown

HOW TO USE THIS GUIDE

The *Truth Plus Love Video Study* is designed to be experienced in a group setting such as a Bible study, Sunday school class, or any small-group gathering. Each session begins with a welcome section, several questions to get you thinking about the topic, and a reading from the Bible. You will then watch a video with Matt Brown and engage in some small-group discussion. You will close each session with a time of personal reflection and prayer as a group.

Each person in the group should have his or her own copy of this study guide. You are also encouraged to have a copy of the *Truth Plus Love* book, as reading the book alongside the curriculum will provide you with deeper insights and make the journey more meaningful. (See the "For Next Week" section at the end of each between-studies section for the chapters in the book that correspond to material you and your group are discussing.)

To get the most out of your group experience, keep the following points in mind. First, the real growth in this study will happen during your small-group time. This is where you will process the content of the teaching for the week, ask questions, and learn from others as you hear what God is doing in their lives. For this reason, it is important for you to be fully committed to the group and attend each session so you can build trust and rapport with the other members. If you choose to only go through the motions, or if you refrain from participating, there is a lesser chance you will find what you're looking for during this study.

Second, remember the goal of your small group is to serve as a place where people can share, learn about God, and build intimacy and friendship. For this reason, seek to make your group a safe place. This means being honest about your thoughts and feelings and listening carefully to everyone else's opinion. (**Note:** *If you are a group leader, there are additional instructions and resources in the back of the book for leading a productive discussion group.*)

Third, resist the temptation to fix a problem someone might be having or to correct his or her theology, as that's not the purpose of your small-group time. Also, keep everything your group shares confidential. This will foster a rewarding sense of community in your group and create a place where people can heal, be challenged, and grow spiritually.

Following your group time, you will have the opportunity to engage the content of *Truth Plus Love* during the week by engaging in any or all of the between-sessions activities. For each session, you may wish to complete the personal study all in one sitting or spread it out over a few days (for example, working on it a half-hour a day on different days that week). Note that if you are unable to finish (or even start!) your between-sessions personal study, you should still attend the group study video session. You are still wanted and welcome at the group even if you don't have your "homework" done.

Keep in mind the videos, discussion questions, and activities are simply meant to kick-start your imagination so you are not only open to what God wants you to hear but also how to apply it to your life. As you go through this study, be watching for what God is saying to you as learn from Jesus' example of how to influence your world through *truth plus love.*

TRUTH *PLUS* JOY

But the fruit of the Spirit is love, **joy**, peace, forbearance,
kindness, goodness, faithfulness, gentleness and self-control.
Against such things there is no law.

GALATIANS 5:22–23

Though you have not seen him, you love him;
and even though you do not see him now, you believe in him and
are filled with an **inexpressible and glorious joy**, for you are receiving
the end result of your faith, the salvation of your souls.

1 PETER 1:8–9

WELCOME

When you first became a follower of Christ, you likely soon discovered there was much to learn. You might have found yourself wanting to know more about the Bible, the principles and promises in it, and how they affected your life. But it wasn't only *information* you craved. You also wanted to grow in the *relationship* you had just started with the living God.

No matter how much you've learned since that time, you've certainly realized there is always more to learn. You've also discovered that God desires more than intellectual comprehension and understanding. He wants you to put into practice what you've learned. He doesn't just want you to "follow the rules" and check off items on a list; rather, he cares about the *attitude* of your heart. He wants you to be "salt and light" to the world around you so that everyone who comes into contact with you knows how much he loves them—so much so that he sent his Son, Jesus, to pay the price for their sins by dying on the cross.

God wants each of us to share the life-changing power of his truth *and* love with those in the world. When we do this—when we live in that place of harmony between truth and love—we will not only reflect God's character but also experience the *joy* and fulfillment for which we were created. God wants us to experience this joy, and when we're in sync with him, we naturally discover the contentment that comes from aligning the truth of his promises with the power of his love. We experience the abundance of his amazing grace.

SHARE

If you or any of your group members are just getting to know one another, take a few minutes to introduce yourselves. Then, to kick things off, discuss the following questions:

✈ What kind of student were you in school? How would your classmates have described you? Quiet and studious? Outgoing and driven by achievements? The teacher's pet? Average and unassuming? Something else?

✈ If the words *truth plus love* describes the Christian life, what two words—*what* plus *what*—describes your feelings as you contemplate starting this study? How do both of those words reflect your expectations?

READ

Invite someone to read aloud the following passage. Listen for fresh insights as you hear the verses being read, and then discuss the questions that follow.

> A farmer went out to sow his seed. As he was scattering the seed, some fell along the path, and the birds came and ate it up. Some fell on rocky places, where it did not have much soil. It sprang up quickly, because the soil was shallow. But when the sun came up, the plants were scorched, and they withered because they had no root. Other seed fell among thorns, which grew up and choked the plants. Still other seed fell on good soil, where it produced a crop—a hundred, sixty or thirty times what was sown. . . .
>
> Listen then to what the parable of the sower means: When anyone hears the message about the kingdom and does not understand it, the evil one comes and snatches away what was sown in their heart. This is the seed sown along the path. The seed falling on rocky ground refers to someone who hears the word and at once receives it with joy. But since they have no root, they last only a short time. When trouble or persecution comes because of the word, they quickly fall away.

The seed falling among the thorns refers to someone who hears the word, but the worries of this life and the deceitfulness of wealth choke the word, making it unfruitful. But the seed falling on good soil refers to someone who hears the word and understands it. This is the one who produces a crop, yielding a hundred, sixty or thirty times what was sown (Matthew 13:3–8, 18–23).

What is one key insight that stands out to you from this passage?

What does the seed represent in this parable? What do the different types of soil represent?

WATCH

Play the video segment for session 1. As you watch, use the following outline to record any thoughts that stand out to you.

Notes

God wants us to have holiness in our lives so we won't hurt ourselves, we won't hurt others, and we will walk in the joy that he has for us . . . this great happiness.

In the first half of Ephesians, Paul only tells his readers to remember what Jesus has done for them. This is the true picture of the Christian life: everything we are called to do is built on the *joy* we have received and what Jesus has done for us.

Jesus tells a story in Matthew 13:1–8 about a farmer who is scattering seeds. The seed lands on different types of soil, which represents the different ways people receive the gospel:

The "rocky soil" people

The "shallow soil" people

The "weedy soil" people

The "good soil" people

The message of the gospel can have a "trickle effect" in the lives of the people around us.

Several obstacles to joy that we might be experiencing in our lives:

#1: The obstacle of comparison

#2: The obstacle of uncertainty and fear

#3: The obstacle of an overburdened schedule

#4: The obstacle of distance from Jesus

Four practical ways you can get your joy back and experience more of the happiness that God wants for you:

#1: Rest and reset your schedule

#2: Plan a party

#3: Make a list of the things for which you're grateful

#4: Remind yourself of the good things God has done

DISCUSS

Take a few minutes with your group members to discuss what you just watched and explore these concepts in Scripture.

1. Read Galatians 5:22–23. Why do you think Paul refers to these as "fruit" of the Spirit? What is required for this fruit to take root and grow in our lives?

2. Read 1 John 3:7–10. Why does God call his followers to pursue holiness? How does pursuing God's holiness lead to joy?

3. What are some of the challenges of sharing the gospel with "rocky soil" type people? With "shallow soil" people? With "weedy soil" people?

4. In what ways has comparing yourself to others, dealing with uncertainty, and having a too-busy schedule stolen your joy?

5. What practical steps can you put in place this week to rest and reset your schedule? What will you do to "plan a party" and just celebrate your life?

6. What are several items you can list right now for which you are thankful? What can you do this week to remind yourself of everything God has done for you?

RESPOND

Briefly review the outline for the video teaching and any notes you took. In the space below, write down the most significant point you took away from this session.

PRAY

Close by praying aloud together for a few minutes, asking God to work in each person's heart as you reflect on what it means to balance *truth plus love* in your life. Write down any specific requests in the space below so you can remember to continue praying throughout the week.

BETWEEN-SESSIONS PERSONAL STUDY

If you haven't already started reading *Truth Plus Love*, now is the perfect time to begin. This week, you might want to read chapters 1–3 before starting this study. Note that the questions and exercises provided in this between-sessions section are not intended to burden you with homework but simply to help you receive the greatest benefit from the content. The three sections are designed to help you understand the big idea (*God's Truth*), reflect and make it your own (*Plus Love*), and put that idea into action (*Equals Influence*). Write your responses and reflections here or in a journal or notebook dedicated to this study. There will be time for you to share your reflections and results at the beginning of the next session.

GOD'S TRUTH

The goal of the Christian life is to become more like Jesus as we experience the fullness of our heavenly Father's love and are empowered by the Holy Spirit. As Paul explained, "Speaking the truth in love, we are to grow up in every way into him who is the head, into Christ" (Ephesians 4:15 ESV). This is Spiritual Maturity 101: Truth + Love = Influence. God calls us to balance both *truth* and *love* without favoring one above the other.

Jesus provides the perfect example of what living out this balance looks like. He was fully human and fully God—and "full of grace and truth" (John 1:14). Jesus lived out his life walking in truth and love, and he calls his followers to do the same. For us, this will require practice. We have to *think about* what it looks like in our everyday lives: in our attitudes, opinions, relationships, interactions, service, leadership, lifestyle, and daily habits. God provides us with new life in Christ, but we still have to do our part. We need to obey God's commands, live according to the principles outlined in Scripture, and advance his kingdom.

"Doing our part" means living in ways that show evidence of God in our lives. This is the "fruit of the Spirit" to which Paul refers in Galatians 5:22–23: "The fruit of the Spirit is love, joy, peace, forbearance, kindness, goodness, faithfulness, gentleness and self-control." Paul adds, "Those who belong to Christ Jesus have crucified the flesh with its passions and desires. Since we live by the Spirit, let us keep in step with the Spirit" (verses 24–25).

Being a follower of Christ means that instead of living for ourselves and our own desires, we live for Jesus and serve others accordingly. This helps us to maintain the balance between truth and love as we "keep in step" with God's Spirit dwelling in us.

Why are both truth and love required for us to grow in our faith? How do the two complement each other? How do they contrast with one another?

Based on what you know about the life of Jesus, what are some examples of the way he balanced truth and love? How did he avoid emphasizing one over the other?

✒ How does cultivating spiritual fruit in our lives promote the balance of truth and love? How do the qualities of love, joy, peace, patience, kindness, goodness, faithfulness, gentleness, and self-control reflect this kind of balanced living?

✒ What does it mean to "keep in step" with God's Spirit? How do you know when you are "out of step" with the Spirit? How do you realign your heart when you get out of step?

PLUS LOVE

The Bible is clear that God values truth and love equally, but as believers it can be difficult to balance the two in our lives. It's easier to err on one side or the other, allowing truth to outweigh love or elevating love at the expense of truth. However, failing to strike this balance can lead to unfortunate consequences for ourselves and others—and rob everyone of joy.

Truth – Love = Noise

In 1 Corinthians 13:1, Paul writes that if we constantly shout the *truth* of God but don't walk in the fullness of his love, we're basically like a toddler banging drums: "If I speak in the tongues of men or of angels, but do not have love, I am only a resounding gong or a clanging cymbal." We're making *noise* but not music—shouting but not being heard because of the way we are delivering the message. As a result, our ability to point others to Christ suffers.

Love − Truth = Error

On the other hand, if we focus solely on the *love* of God but fail to proclaim his truth to others, we lose the power to save. The authors of the Bible clearly warn us against this error: "I say this because some ungodly people have wormed their way into your churches, saying that God's marvelous grace allows us to live immoral lives. The condemnation of such people was recorded long ago, for they have denied our only Master and Lord, Jesus Christ" (Jude 4 NLT).

The good news of the gospel is clear: "All have sinned and fall short of the glory of God, and all are justified freely by his grace through the redemption that came by Christ Jesus" (Romans 3:23–24). We are *all* sinners and are only saved by grace through faith in Jesus. When we repent and accept this gift of grace, we are then called to obey God and follow Jesus' example. We are called to be active participants and not just spectators—true followers and not just fans. God loves us as we are, but he loves us too much to leave us where we are.

Think of times you've focused more on sharing God's truth but not his love. How did others react to what you shared? What motivated you to share in the way you did? How were you aware of lacking love to balance out the truth?

✖ Now think of a few times you compromised or ignored the truth and focused only on love as you interacted with others. What influenced you to act this way? How aware were you of allowing love to outweigh truth?

✖ Do you naturally tend to emphasize truth more or love more? How does this natural tendency manifest itself in you and your interactions with others?

✖ The Bible states that "the joy of the LORD is your strength" (Nehemiah 8:10). What are some things that tend to rob you of joy—and God's strength in your life?

EQUALS INFLUENCE

God doesn't just want to save your soul. He also wants to make you holy—to transform your character and your inner life to reflect that of Christ. He wants you to be "the light of the world" so that you can shine the light of Christ "before others, that they may see your good deeds and glorify your Father in heaven" (Matthew 5:14, 16). Striking the balance between truth and love thus allows you to reflect his character and influence the world. In other words, *Truth (the Gospel) + Love (the Fruit of the Spirit) = Influence.*

A Personal Assessment

Use the following list to conduct a personal inventory of the spiritual fruit in your life. For each item, write down a number between *1* and *5*, with *1* indicating "absent in my life / needs work" and *5* indicating "abundant in my life / overflowing." As you do this, don't be too hard on yourself or use the exercise as a tool to beat yourself up for what you "should" be seeing in your life. Just be gracious with yourself and ask the Holy Spirit to lead you.

___ Love	___ Joy	___ Peace
___ Patience	___ Kindness	___ Goodness
___ Faithfulness	___ Gentleness	___ Self-Control

Now try to recall a recent example of when you displayed each trait. Briefly write down the situation and your response.

Love

Joy

Peace

Patience

Kindness

Goodness

Faithfulness

Gentleness

Self-Control

As you look at your list, try to notice any patterns. Look at which spiritual fruits seem to come more naturally for you and which ones are more difficult for you to express.

Overcoming Joy Blockers

During the teaching this week, you were given four ways to get your joy back and experience more of the happiness in life that God wants you to have. In the space below, write down some practical steps you have taken (or will take) to put these into effect in your life.

- What are some ways you have taken time to *rest and reset your schedule*? What items have you prioritized? How has this affected your level of joy?

- What are some ways you have *celebrated life*? If you didn't throw an actual party, what else did you do to get together with friends? How has this affected your joy?

- Did you take time to *make a list* of twenty to thirty things for which you are grateful? Was that easy or difficult for you to do? Why do you feel this was the case?

What are some ways you reminded your heart of all the good things that God has done for you? What passages of Scripture help to remind you of God's goodness?

RECOMMENDED READING

In preparation for session 2, read chapter 4 in *Truth Plus Love*. Use the space below to note any key points or questions you want to share at the beginning of your next group meeting.

SESSION TWO

TRUTH

PEACE

I have told you these things, so that in me **you may have peace**.
In this world you will have trouble. But take heart!
I have overcome the world.

JOHN 16:33

Do not repay anyone evil for evil. Be careful to do what is right
in the eyes of everyone. If it is possible, as far as it depends on you,
live at peace with everyone.

ROMANS 12:17–18

WELCOME

What comes to mind when you think back on your days in high school? Perhaps you look back with fond memories of your classes, your teachers, and the other students at the school. Or maybe you get a feeling of dread when you think back on those days—and you are glad they are behind you. Or, like most of us, perhaps you fall somewhere in between.

Regardless, there was one phrase that no high-school student ever wanted to hear: "It's time for a *pop quiz*." Those two dreaded words . . . *pop* . . . *quiz* . . . could fill even the stoutest heart with anxiety. *Did I do my homework? Did I actually read that chapter in the textbook? Did I pay enough attention in class? How much will this be worth on my final grade?*

Each of us at times will experience our own versions of "pop quizzes" in life. None of us knows what is going to happen tomorrow—and this world has proven to be a place where crises can arise at a moment's notice. It is for this reason the Bible tells us to have the *peace of God*. This is a peace that allows us to be calm and remain confident that God will take care of us even in the midst of the worst circumstances of our lives.

It is so important for us to have this kind of peace because it not only allows us to *tell* people the truth that God is in control but also to *show* them we believe that truth through the way we lead our lives. When we demonstrate we understand God's *truth* plus his *peace,* we become a strong influence for Christ and serve to draw others to him.

SHARE

If you or any of your group members are just meeting for the first time, take a few minutes to introduce yourselves and share any insights you have from last week's personal study. Next, to kick things off for the group time, discuss the following questions:

✈ What are some "pop quiz" moments that you have experienced—challenges that seemed to come out of nowhere to disrupt your life?

✈ When are you most at peace in your life? What are some activities you like to do that bring you the most peace?

READ

Invite someone to read aloud the following passage. Listen for fresh insights as you hear the verses being read, and then discuss the questions that follow.

> *Rejoice in the Lord always. I will say it again: Rejoice! Let your gentleness be evident to all. The Lord is near. Do not be anxious about anything, but in every situation, by prayer and petition, with thanksgiving, present your requests to God. And the peace of God, which transcends all understanding, will guard your hearts and your minds in Christ Jesus.*
>
> *Finally, brothers and sisters, whatever is true, whatever is noble, whatever is right, whatever is pure, whatever is lovely, whatever is admirable—if anything is excellent or praiseworthy—think about such things. Whatever you have learned or received or heard from me, or seen in me—put it into practice. And the God of peace will be with you* (Philippians 4:4–9).

What is one key insight that stands out to you from this passage?

What does Paul say you should do when you feel anxious and need God's peace?

WATCH

Play the video segment for session 2. As you watch, use the following outline to record any thoughts that stand out to you.

Notes

There is no lasting peace in our lives outside of the gospel of Jesus Christ. There was no other way to peace but through what Jesus did for us on the cross.

Two dramatic stories about the peace of God:

Steve McQueen

Louis Zamperini

Three types of peace that God brings into our lives:

#1: Peace with God

#2: The peace of God

Christians can be calm in a crazy world

We sometimes need to pray for peace

#3: Peace with others

Don't respond to everything

Focus on what is praiseworthy

Become known for what you're for

Have more grace when you do disagree with people

Some practical ways to be a peacemaker this week:

#1: Spend time in solitude

#2: Watch your words you speak to others

#3: Review recent social media posts

#4: Reconcile with another person

DISCUSS

Take a few minutes with your group members to discuss what you just watched and explore these concepts in Scripture.

1. Read Ephesians 2:13–17. How does Paul describe Jesus in this passage? What does he say was one of Jesus' purposes in coming into this world?

2. What does it mean to have peace *with* God? How should that lead to having the peace *of* God in your life?

3. Read John 16:31–33. What does Jesus promise to his followers in this passage? How can this help you to remain calm in a crazy world?

4. How can focusing on what is praiseworthy bring peace into your life? What are some ways you might extend grace to people when you disagree with them?

5. What are some of the ways that you seek to be a peacemaker? Which of the ways mentioned in the teaching especially resonated with you? Why?

6. Who are some people you know whose lives were radically changed when they came to follow Christ? How did the peace of God change their attitudes and actions?

RESPOND

Briefly review the outline for the video teaching and any notes you took. In the space below, write down the most significant point you took away from this session.

PRAY

Finish your group session by praying together, thanking God for his mercy and asking him to bring peace into the life of any member who is feeling anxious this week. Write down specific requests in the space below so you can remember to continue praying throughout the week.

BETWEEN-SESSIONS PERSONAL STUDY

The following questions and exercises on the *peace of God* will again help you apply this week's teaching and practice the personal application. Before you begin, you might want to finish reading chapters 3–4 in *Truth Plus Love*. As you consider how to experience the power of God's peace in your life more fully, reflect on your responses and ask the Holy Spirit to guide you toward the next steps. You can write your responses and reflections in the space provided or in the journal or notebook you started last time. Once again, there will be time for you to share your observations and outcomes at the beginning of the next session.

GOD'S TRUTH

What stands out the most to you as you think about your last group session? What area of your life do you sense God calling you to address to restore a balance between truth and love? Spend a few moments quieting your heart before God, and then read through the following passage from Psalm 46:1–3:

> God is our refuge and strength,
>   an ever-present help in trouble.
> Therefore we will not fear, though the earth give way
>   and the mountains fall into the heart of the sea,
> though its waters roar and foam
>   and the mountains quake with their surging.

Which words and images contrast the most in this passage? How does this reinforce the central message that you need not fear because God is always in control?

Why do you think the psalmist emphasizes God is "an ever-present help" during calamitous times? What is the implication about our human tendencies to be afraid when the storms of life—either literally or figuratively—crash around us?

How does this passage reflect the supernatural essence of God's peace? When have you experienced this kind of peace—the kind that defies logic based on circumstances?

How would you rewrite or paraphrase this passage in your own words? Try not to use the words in this translation and instead draw from your personal experience. What images or descriptive words come to mind to express your experience?

PLUS LOVE

When you accepted Christ into your life, your heart was flooded with his peace. This is a peace *with* God that came about because of your reconciliation with your Creator. Nonetheless, there will be times when you will still drift into worry, anxiety, and fear. In those moments, the Bible calls you to experience what is known as the peace *of* God. This is a type of peace that will "guard your hearts and your minds in Christ Jesus" (Philippians 4:7).

God's peace will guard your heart and your mind against the attacks of the enemy. It will enable you to "take captive every thought to make it obedient to Christ" (2 Corinthians 10:5). You can access this peace simply by remaining aware of God's presence and calling on him for help. He will grant you his peace when you exercise your faith in him and trust in him.

The prophet Isaiah said of God, "You will keep in perfect peace those whose minds are steadfast, because they trust in you" (26:3). So, if you need more of God's peace in your life, come back to child-like trust in his care for you. "Let the peace of Christ rule in your hearts" (Colossians 3:15), and "cast all your anxiety on him because he cares for you" (1 Peter 5:7).

When have you most recently felt an overwhelming sense of God's peace in your life? How did this help you at the time? How did this affect those around you?

When have you most recently experienced a battle with fear, anxiety, or worry? What events or conversations triggered this reaction?

How did this influence your interactions with others? Looking back, how do you wish you had responded differently?

SESSION TWO: **TRUTH PLUS PEACE**

✈ What obstacles and stressors typically interfere and rob you of experiencing God's peace? Check all the possibilities below that apply, and feel free to add your own:

____ Health concerns
____ Stress at work
____ Bills and debts
____ Fears about the future
____ Grudges from the past
____ Worries related to family
____ Expectations from others around you
____ Current events and world news
____ Strife at home
____ Envying friends
____ Regrets over past mistakes
____ Emotional wounds from the past
____ Others:

Look over the items you checked. Spend a few moments in prayer, lifting up each item and trusting God to take care of it. Breathe in the relief that comes from surrendering to his control, and ask him to restore his peace in all areas of your life.

EQUALS INFLUENCE

In addition to experiencing the fullness of God's peace in your own life, the Bible also calls you to walk in peace with the world around you. You are actually *commanded* to bring peace wherever you go: "Make every effort to live in peace with everyone and to be holy; without holiness no one will see the Lord" (Hebrews 12:14). But to do this, you first need to experience the inner calm that comes from having God's peace within your own heart. This may require you to ask someone to forgive you for the way you've treated him or her in the past, or it might mean you need to forgive someone who has hurt you (see Colossians 3:13).

This may also require you to recharge your battery and detox from the stress, noise, and busyness that will often threaten to consume your inner peace. One of the best and simplest ways to do this is to unplug from technology for a time—no social media, headlines, texts, articles, podcasts, news notifications, TV reports, or other news media sources. Consider making this your personal challenge this week by engaging in one of the following:

- Choose one full day—your own personal "Sabbath"—to unplug. This could be Sunday or any other day in the week you choose for this personal "fast."

- Choose a set time of day, such as morning or evening, to forego accessing media and going online. Focus instead on spending time in prayer, in Bible study, or in interacting with your family and loved ones.

- Think about the news feed or social media site that tends to cause you the most anxiety and unrest, and choose to fast from accessing it this week.

In addition to limiting your online presence and news intake, pay attention to the words you use in conversation, in texts, on social media, and in comments to others' social media posts. Does the way you communicate bring peace to those who read your words? Or are you sowing seeds of strife, whether intentionally or not, through a critical spirit or negative attitude? Consider practicing a positive response—or no response at all—for one whole day. Try to make this a habit so you can more actively share God's peace with others.

✈ Which of the options did you select? What were some of the challenges in unplugging from news feeds and social media?

✈ What did you choose to do instead with this time? What was the result?

✈ How did this exercise help you to focus more on God and experience his peace?

RECOMMENDED READING

In preparation for session 3, read chapter 5 in *Truth Plus Love*. Use the space below to note any key points or questions you want to share at the beginning of your next group meeting.

TRUTH
PLUS
GENTLENESS

Take my yoke upon you and learn from me,
for I am **gentle and humble in heart**, and you will find rest for
your souls. For my yoke is easy and my burden is light.

MATTHEW 11:29–30

Be kind to one another, **tender-hearted**, forgiving each other,
just as God in Christ also has forgiven you.

EPHESIANS 4:32 (NASB)

WELCOME

If you played an instrument growing up, you likely remember the first time you picked it up and decided it was something you wanted to learn. At first, your instructor had you focus on studying just the notes and playing them in the right order. It wasn't until later, after you gained proficiency with the instrument, that you began to play those notes at the correct tempo (fast or slow) and volume (loud or soft).

Once you learned these techniques, you were on your way to actually playing *music*. The same can be said of your Christian life. When you first became a believer, you likely focused on just learning the Word of God—what it said and what it meant to you. But over time, as you developed in your spiritual maturity, you learned how to apply those truths in the way you think, speak, and interact with others. You learned the importance of not only expressing God's *truth* but also reflecting God's *love* through kindness and gentleness.

Paul drew on this same kind of musical imagery when he wrote, "If I speak in the tongues of men or angels, but do not have love, I am only a resounding gong or a clanging symbol" (1 Corinthians 13:1). The way people perceive Christ will always be colored by the attitudes and actions of his followers. If they see believers engaging in criticism, judgment, and anger, it will be difficult for them to perceive God as a loving heavenly Father. But if they see Christians extending grace, mercy, and forgiveness, it will draw them to God.

If we want to be passionate about the truth of God's Word, then we must also be passionate about God's commands to extend kindness and gentleness. The love of God shines through in the way we treat one another.

SHARE

Begin your group time by inviting anyone to share his or her insights from last week's personal study. Next, to kick things off for the group time, discuss the following questions:

What are some ways that you like to extend kindness and gentleness to others? What impact have you seen from your actions?

When was the last time a stranger showed you a kindness that made a difference in your day? Why did it have such a memorable impact?

READ

Invite someone to read aloud the following passage. Listen for fresh insights as you hear the verses being read, and then discuss the questions that follow.

> *Do not lie to each other, since you have taken off your old self with its practices and have put on the new self, which is being renewed in knowledge in the image of its Creator. Here there is no Gentile or Jew, circumcised or uncircumcised, barbarian, Scythian, slave or free, but Christ is all, and is in all.*
>
> *Therefore, as God's chosen people, holy and dearly loved, clothe yourselves with compassion, kindness, humility, gentleness and patience. Bear with each other and forgive one another if any of you has a grievance against someone. Forgive as the Lord forgave you. And over all these virtues put on love, which binds them all together in perfect unity.*
>
> *Let the peace of Christ rule in your hearts, since as members of one body you were called to peace. And be thankful. Let the message of Christ dwell among you richly as you teach and admonish*

*one another with all wisdom through psalms, hymns, and songs
from the Spirit, singing to God with gratitude in your hearts. And
whatever you do, whether in word or deed, do it all in the name
of the Lord Jesus, giving thanks to God the Father through him*
(Colossians 3:9–17).

What is one key insight that stands out to you from this passage?

What do you think it means to "clothe" yourself with compassion
and gentleness?

WATCH

Play the video segment for session 3. As you watch, use the following outline to record any thoughts that stand out to you.

Notes

Paul says in Galatians 5:23 that *gentleness* is one of the fruits of the
Spirit that God works into our lives. It is a part of the process of us
growing in spiritual maturity.

Two key biblical themes regarding gentleness:

#1: Gentleness is to be a *defining characteristic* of our Christian lives. We are to put on gentleness like we put on our clothes (see Colossians 3:12).

#2: We are called to *sound different* from those in the world. We have been set apart for the ways God wants us to speak and live and talk (see 2 Timothy 2:23 and Ephesians 4:29).

Several obstacles to gentleness that we might encounter:

#1: The obstacle of the wrong view of spiritual maturity

#2: The obstacle of living in a harsh world

#3: The obstacle of our twenty-four-hour news media

#4: The obstacle of not having enough margin

Five practical ways you can grow in your gentleness toward others:

#1: Give yourself more margin in your calendar

#2: Turn off the news this week

#3: Learn from someone who demonstrates gentleness

#4: Apologize to anyone you have wronged

#5: Share hard truths with incredible gentleness

God has called us to walk in his *truth plus gentleness*—and that starts in our own homes with our own families, because that is the most difficult place to walk it out.

DISCUSS

Take a few minutes with your group members to discuss what you just watched and explore these concepts in Scripture.

1. Read 1 Peter 3:15–16. How does Peter say that you are to present the truth of the gospel to others? Why do you think he stresses the need for gentleness and respect?

2. Read Ephesians 4:29–32. Why is it important for us to display gentleness in our communications with others? In what ways is this a challenge for you?

3. How has God helped you to understand that being compassionate, caring, and gentle toward others is a vital component of your spiritual maturity? How has that helped you to be kinder and more considerate in an often harsh and critical world?

4. Read Titus 3:1–2. How have you seen social media used as a means to slander others and disrespect those in authority? Why is it important to demonstrate gentleness and consideration toward others, even in our social media posts?

SESSION THREE: **TRUTH PLUS GENTLENESS**

5. What are some of the ways that you seek to continually grow in demonstrating *truth plus gentleness* in your life?

6. Which of the ideas mentioned in the teaching for growing in kindness and gentleness especially resonated with you? Why?

RESPOND

Briefly review the outline for the video teaching and any notes you took. In the space below, write down the most significant point you took away from this session.

PRAY

As you close your group session, share one area in which you would like to practice gentleness more consistently—whether at home, at work, at school, or with certain difficult people in your life. Pray together as a group for these requests, and then write down any other needs that are brought up in the space below so you can continue to pray for them during the week.

BETWEEN-SESSIONS PERSONAL STUDY

As the apostle Paul notes in Galatians 5:22–23, both *kindness* and *gentleness*—the focus of this week's study—are fruits of the Spirit that can help you grow in Christ and become more spiritually mature. Before you begin, you might want to finish reading chapter 5 in *Truth Plus Love*. Once again, record your responses and reflections in the space provided or in a journal and consider sharing your observations with the group at the beginning of the next session.

GOD'S TRUTH

As a follower of Christ, being kind and gentle is not an option but a *command*. We are to "be kind and compassionate to one another, forgiving each other, just as in Christ God forgave you" (Ephesians 4:32). God wants us to be forgiving, kind, and gentle toward others because he has been that way with us—"God demonstrates his own love for us in this: While we were still sinners, Christ died for us" (Romans 5:8). We deserved to face the punishment of death for our sins, but God "so loved the world that he gave his one and only Son, that whoever believes in him shall not perish but have eternal life" (John 3:16).

Our kindness and gentleness should *define* us to those around us. Unfortunately, the sad truth is that many Christians today have become known more for what they are *against* than for what they are *for*. We need to do our best to reverse this trend and show everyone the goodness and graciousness of God's lovingkindness toward all people—not just the ones we like, or who agree with us, or who we can understand.

This struggle to show kindness is nothing new. During Jesus' time on earth, an expert in the law once asked him how he could inherit eternal life. Jesus responded by asking the man what was written in the Law. Of course, the expert knew the right answer and gave it, quoting both Deuteronomy 6:5 and Leviticus 19:18 to show how God commanded his people to love their neighbors as themselves. But the expert then went on to ask, "Who is my neighbor?" Instead of giving the man a direct answer:

> In reply Jesus said: "A man was going down from Jerusalem to Jericho, when he was attacked by robbers. They stripped him of his clothes, beat him and went away, leaving him half dead. A priest happened to be going down the same road, and when he saw the man, he passed by on the other side. So too, a Levite, when he came to the place and saw him, passed by on the other side. But a Samaritan, as he traveled, came where the man was; and when he saw him, he took pity on him. He went to him and bandaged his wounds, pouring on oil and wine. Then he put the man on his own donkey, brought him to an inn and took care of him. The next day he took out two denarii and gave them to the innkeeper. 'Look after him,' he said, 'and when I return, I will reimburse you for any extra expense you may have.'
>
> "Which of these three do you think was a neighbor to the man who fell into the hands of robbers?"
>
> The expert in the law replied, "The one who had mercy on him."
> Jesus told him, "Go and do likewise" (Luke 10:30–37).

Why did the expert in the law ask Jesus to identify his "neighbor"? How was he testing Jesus by asking this question? How would *you* have answered the man?

- Why do you think Jesus told the story of the "Good Samaritan" instead of directly responding to the expert in the law?

- How did this story serve to answer the man's question better than if Jesus had simply stated, "Everyone is your neighbor"?

- What acts of kindness did the Samaritan do for the man who had been left for dead by the robbers? Make a brief list of each act you see in the passage.

✘ What did it cost the Samaritan in terms of time and money to stop and help the man? What is Jesus implying it will cost *us* to extend his kindness toward others?

PLUS LOVE

It's not only our *actions* that reflect our gentleness as believers but also our *words*. As Christians, we are to "encourage one another and build each other up" (1 Thessalonians 5:11) and to not "let any unwholesome talk" come out of our mouths (Ephesians 4:29). In an age filled with constant criticism and online trolling—where virtually everyone assumes the right to express his or her own opinions—we are to exhibit the fruit of kindness.

The apostle Paul explains how we can do this: "Don't get involved in foolish, ignorant arguments that only start fights. A servant of the Lord must not quarrel but must be kind to everyone, be able to teach, and be patient with difficult people. Gently instruct those who oppose the truth. Perhaps God will change those people's hearts, and they will learn the truth" (2 Timothy 2:23–25 NLT). As followers of Jesus, we're set apart from the world and the way others act and are called to a higher standard than our egos and self-pride. "We are therefore Christ's ambassadors" (2 Corinthians 5:20). What we say, and how we say it, matters.

This includes how we interact with other believers. Sadly, while most Christians would declare they are adamantly against hypocrisy and deceitfulness, they think nothing of posting biting comments or hateful responses online. But God says unkind speech is never acceptable! Kindness isn't just an extracurricular trait that is nice to have—it is an indispensable trait God commands us to display in both our walk and our talk.

🕊 Think through your social media posts lately, your comments with coworkers, and your conversations with family and friends. How would others describe the tone and style of those recent communications? Is this how you want to come across?

🕊 More importantly, is this how God wants you to reflect his character to others? Why or why not?

🕊 How much time do you spend, either online or in person, complaining about problems? How often do you criticize people? What inaccurate message are you sending others about what it means to follow Christ?

✈ When was the last time you spoke words of kindness and appreciation to your close friends? What could you do today to show your love and support of them?

✈ When was the last time you called (not texted) your parents or siblings just to tell them you love them? How do you think hearing that from you would impact them?

✈ How often do you show your coworkers, especially team members in supporting roles, that you're grateful for their help? What is one creative idea for showing your appreciation to a fellow worker that you could implement this week?

During the next week, try to be mindful of what you're saying and how you are saying it. Pay attention to others, really listen to them, and respond in thoughtful ways (see James 1:19). Use the acronym **T-H-I-N-K** before you speak—is it true, honorable, important, necessary, kind?

EQUALS INFLUENCE

Paul notes that we are to "outdo one another in showing honor" (Romans 12:10 ESV). When we honor people by listening to their stories or praising them and their work, we open the door to sharing about our relationship with God. Honoring others gives us greater influence with them because they know we respect them and care about what's important to them. Just think what an impression we would leave if we actually *competed* to bless, serve, and honor others. What kind of an impact would that have on a person who was in need of Christ?

With this in mind, come up with a plan before your next group meeting to honor someone you especially appreciate right now. The way you show your honor should be personal and appropriate to your relationship. The goal is not to embarrass the person or to highlight your own generosity or kindness. (You might even consider honoring him or her in a way others would not know about.) Make the way you honor this person sacrificial by going out of your way and doing something you would not normally do.

If you need some ideas, here are a few possibilities drawn from *Truth Plus Love*:

- Honor teachers, coaches, or mentors in your community for their investment in children and young people by gifting them with new equipment, money for a scholarship fund, or volunteer service.

- Honor families with young kids at your church by planning and coordinating a fun event so parents can enjoy a date night or evening alone.

- Honor veterans and those in the armed forces by supporting a local ministry that provides food, counseling, and job training for them and their families.

- Honor your pastor and church staff by writing a card or letter describing what you especially appreciate about the way they serve your church.

- Honor your parents or the loving caregivers who were instrumental to your childhood faith by planning a surprise visit or time to catch up together. If too much distance separates you, consider a half-hour video call.

- Honor your spouse or children by turning off your phone the next time you have an opportunity to have a conversation. Don't tell them you're doing it—just show them how engaged you are with them and what's on their hearts.

In the space below, write down what you will do this week to honor another person.

Now record the impact your actions had on that individual and what you took away from the experience.

RECOMMENDED READING

In preparation for session 4, read chapter 6 in *Truth Plus Love*. Use the space below to note any key points or questions you want to share at the beginning of your next group meeting.

TRUTH
PLUS
FAITHFULNESS

One who is **faithful** in a very little is also **faithful** in much, and one who is dishonest in a very little is also dishonest in much.

LUKE 16:10 (ESV)

Happy are those who remain **faithful** under trials, because when they succeed in passing such a test, they will receive as their reward the life which God has promised to those who love him.

JAMES 1:12 (GNT)

WELCOME

Perhaps you were the athletic type growing up. You loved playing sports such as baseball, basketball, or football. You enjoyed the anticipation leading up to a big game, hearing the roar of the crowd when you took the field, and even the smell of the popcorn and hot dogs from the concession stands. But one thing you certainly learned is that to be a success in your sport took work—a lot of *hard* work. It wasn't enough to just talk a big game. You had to faithfully show up for practices, continually work to improve, and even study the other team's weaknesses.

The same is true of our lives in Christ. It's not enough for us to just "talk the talk" and say that we want to do great things for others. No, we are called to also "walk the walk" by continually showing up to serve others in *truth plus love*. It's our acts of continual faithfulness—no matter how great or small—that will speak volumes to others. When people perceive that believers in Christ faithfully follow through on the commitments and promises they make, it will be attractive to them and motivate them to seek out Christ as well.

The Bible makes it clear "it is by grace [we] have been saved" and not through any of the good works we have done (Ephesians 2:8). Yet God's Word is equally clear that we are called to do our part to serve others in God's kingdom. As Paul continued, "We are God's handiwork, created in Christ Jesus to do good works, which God prepared in advance for us to do" (2:10). God saves us through his amazing grace even as he allows us to participate in the good works that he is accomplishing for all people. We walk in *truth plus faithfulness*.

SHARE

Begin your group time by inviting anyone to share his or her insights from last week's personal study. Next, to kick things off for the group time, discuss the following questions:

🕊 What are some of the challenges you face when it comes to faithfulness? How have you sought to overcome those obstacles in your life?

🕊 Why is it important to not only "talk the talk" when it comes to sharing about Christ with others but also to "walk the walk"?

READ

Invite someone to read aloud the following passage. Listen for fresh insights as you hear the verses being read, and then discuss the questions that follow.

> *Then the Kingdom of Heaven will be like ten bridesmaids who took their lamps and went to meet the bridegroom. Five of them were foolish, and five were wise. The five who were foolish didn't take enough olive oil for their lamps, but the other five were wise enough to take along extra oil. When the bridegroom was delayed, they all became drowsy and fell asleep.*
>
> *At midnight they were roused by the shout, "Look, the bridegroom is coming! Come out and meet him!"*
>
> *All the bridesmaids got up and prepared their lamps. Then the five foolish ones asked the others, "Please give us some of your oil because our lamps are going out."*
>
> *But the others replied, "We don't have enough for all of us. Go to a shop and buy some for yourselves."*
>
> *But while they were gone to buy oil, the bridegroom came. Then those who were ready went in with him to the marriage feast,*

and the door was locked. Later, when the other five bridesmaids returned, they stood outside, calling, "Lord! Lord! Open the door for us!"

But he called back, "Believe me, I don't know you!"

So you, too, must keep watch! For you do not know the day or hour of my return (Matthew 25:1–13 NLT).

What is one key insight that stands out to you from this passage?

What does this parable say about the need to be faithful to Jesus?

WATCH

Play the video segment for session 4. As you watch, use the following outline to record any thoughts that stand out to you.

Notes

God saves us just as we are—we don't have to "get right" first to come to God. We come as we are to God our Father . . . but he doesn't *leave us* as we are.

Even with all our science, and all our data, and all of technology, and all our advancements, we all still struggle with the basic problem of the sinfulness of our own hearts.

Two stories of people in previous generations who exhibited great faithfulness:

Henry Brown, the first Mennonite missionary to China

Mark and Shirley Denyes, who came through incredibly difficult circumstances

Several ways that you can grown in your faithfulness:

#*1:* Focus on being faithful in the little things

#*2:* Focus on who you are when no one is watching

#*3:* Focus on keeping your word

#*4:* Focus on tuning in to God

#*5:* Focus on the long game

Four practical ways you can walk in faithfulness this week:

#*1:* Read the Bible

#2: Spend time with someone who demonstrates faithfulness

#3: Find a place to serve in your church

#4: Spend time meditating on the faithfulness of God

DISCUSS

Take a few minutes with your group members to discuss what you just watched and explore these concepts in Scripture.

1. Read James 1:22–24. How does James describe a person who "talks the talk" but doesn't "walk the walk"? What role does faithfulness play in this?

2. Who are some individuals you know who have demonstrated faithfulness? What particular lessons did you learn from their example?

3. Read Matthew 25:21. Why is it important to be faithful in the little things in life? How does God reward such faithfulness?

4. Read Matthew 6:1. What does Jesus say in this verse about your motives when it comes to serving others? How does God want you to practice faithfulness?

5. Read Galatians 6:9. When is it the most difficult for you to remain committed to something you've agreed to do? What encouragement does this verse offer?

6. What are some of the ways that you seek to continually grow in *truth plus faithfulness* in your life? Which of the ideas mentioned in the teaching for growing in kindness and faithfulness especially resonated with you? Why?

RESPOND

Briefly review the outline for the video teaching and any notes you took. In the space below, write down the most significant point you took away from this session.

PRAY

Go around the group and have the group members share a request that is burdening their heart. As you pray together, trust that God hears your prayers, knows your struggles, and will meet your needs according to his wisdom and timing. Silently choose at least one person's request to lift up each day this week until your next group meeting. Write down those requests in the space below so you can remember to pray throughout the week.

BETWEEN-SESSIONS PERSONAL STUDY

God calls you as his follower to not just *talk about* his love but to *demonstrate* his love through faithful acts of service to others. You are to "not love with words or speech but with actions and in truth" (1 John 3:18). As you do this, you will grow in faithfulness and goodness. With this in mind, you might want to finish reading chapter 6 in *Truth Plus Love* before you begin this study. Record your responses and reflections and consider sharing your observations with the group at the beginning of the next session.

GOD'S TRUTH

It can often seem difficult to practice faithfulness and goodness in the midst of so much pain and suffering in our world. Though God is always good, everything in this life certainly isn't, and you will experience trials at times. The enemy of your soul loves to ignite pain and hardship into your days by doing what he does best: lying, deceiving, stealing, killing, and destroying the trust you want to have with God (see John 8:44).

It is important to remember, however, that the presence of pain in this world doesn't mean that God is absent. Pain just proves how much you need to invite God into your world! You can trust him with everything that happens in this life, even if you don't understand how it fits into his divine plan. As Paul writes:

> God causes everything to work together for the good of those who love God and are called according to his purpose for them (Romans 8:28 NLT).

Even in the midst of pain and adversity, God is always working for your good. The Bible even states that God's goodness will follow you all of the days of your life (see Psalm 23:6). Furthermore, when you experience God's blessings and trust him in every circumstance—no matter how difficult—you reflect the goodness and faithfulness of his character:

> His divine power has given us everything we need for a godly life through our knowledge of him who called us by his own glory and goodness. Through these he has given us his very great and precious promises, so that through them you may participate in the divine nature, having escaped the corruption in the world caused by evil desires. For this very reason, make every effort to add to your faith goodness; and to goodness, knowledge; and to knowledge, self-control; and to self-control, perseverance; and to perseverance, godliness; and to godliness, mutual affection; and to mutual affection, love (2 Peter 1:3–7).

How does God's power give you all you need to live a godly life? What role does your knowledge of God and his goodness play in your ability to be obedient to his Word?

How does knowing and claiming God's promises lead to greater spiritual maturity? How do God's promises help you escape "the corruption in the world caused by evil desires"?

Consider the way each quality listed in 2 Peter 1:5–7 contributes to the way you grow and mature in faith. How have you seen each pairing at work in your own personal journey?

Faith + Goodness

Goodness + Knowledge

Knowledge + Self-control

Self-control + Perseverance

Perseverance + Godliness

Godliness + Mutual Affection

Mutual Affection + Love

✦ How does this progression work to strengthen your faith? How does this progression help you balance *truth plus love*?

✦ Which pairing might need more attention for you to reinforce the impact of faithfulness and goodness in your life?

PLUS LOVE

In recent years, people have become more interested in learning about their ancestry and genealogy, thanks to the rise of online sites such as ancestry.com and 23andMe.com. Yet as fascinating as it may be to learn about your physical heritage, it is even more vital to consider your *spiritual* heritage. For instance, you likely inherited many of your ideas about God from your ancestors—your parents and your grandparents. In many ways, you are the product of their spiritual choices and the link to the faith of your future descendants.

It can be encouraging to look back at the stories of some of the "heroes of the faith" in your family. Often, you will find they experienced many of the same trials you are facing. You may be able to trace how answers to their prayers led others to finding Christ.

You can be encouraged in your own life by witnessing the way their faith sustained them in difficult times.

When you can identify the blessings of God across generations, you get a glimpse of the bigger picture revealed by such a legacy of faithfulness and are inspired to do the same in your life. Your words, actions, and decisions will always have consequences that reach far into the future. Your choices will always affect others. So, when you choose to walk in faithfulness and goodness, you will influence your family, your circle of friends, their families, and the generations to come. Walking in faithfulness and goodness will echo throughout eternity.

What stories have been passed down to you about the faithfulness of your family members? What did you personally learn from those stories?

How have those accounts affected your life and the choices you've made to follow God?

✦ Which person in your family tree had the greatest impact on the faith of other members? How so?

✦ What evidence of spiritual fruit do you see in that person's life?

✦ How will *your* descendants look back at your life and see evidence of your faithfulness and goodness? What habits and spiritual disciplines are you currently pursuing as an investment in the spiritual legacy you want to leave?

🪰 What truths from God's Word have sustained you during tough times? Which ones would you want your great-great-grand-children to discover in the future?

🪰 How would you explain the significance of these truths to them if you could?

EQUALS INFLUENCE

"Every good and perfect gift is from above, coming down from the Father of the heavenly lights" (James 1:17). Whether it's your ability to read the words on this page or the taste of your favorite chocolate, the sound of a child's voice or the texture of your dog's fur, the beauty of a sunrise on the beach or the scent of summer honeysuckle, you experience God's good gifts every moment of every day. In fact, his goodness is experienced by all—those who choose to love and serve him as well as those who choose to reject him (see Matthew 5:44–45).

God is gracious and generous in this regard—but it is clear he reserves even more goodness for those who love him. As David wrote, "How great is the goodness you have stored up for those who fear you . . . you lavish it on those who come to you for protection, blessing them before the watching world" (Psalm 31:19 NLT). God is truly good, and he works all things together in your life for good. And because he calls you to follow after him, you should likewise strive to demonstrate goodness and faithfulness in your life (see 1 Corinthians 1:9).

Before your next group meeting, contact someone in your group and make a plan to meet for coffee or a meal. During your time together, consider doing the following:

- Discuss the habits, practices, and spiritual disciplines you have each adopted that help you grow in your faith.

- Share at least one prayer request that is heavy on your heart and commit to faithfully and regularly praying for each other.

- Think about ways you can continue to serve and encourage each other as you seek to balance *truth plus love* in your life.

In the space below, write down some the key habits, practices, and spiritual disciples you discussed that have helped each of you to grow in your faith.

Now write down some of the ways you discussed to continue to serve and encourage each other.

RECOMMENDED READING

In preparation for session 5, read chapter 7 in *Truth Plus Love*. Use the space below to note any key points or questions you want to share at the beginning of your next group meeting.

TRUTH
PLUS
PATIENCE

Love is **patient**, love is kind. It does not envy,
it does not boast, it is not proud. . . . It always protects,
always trusts, always hopes, **always perseveres**.

1 CORINTHIANS 13:4, 7

We do not want you to become lazy, but to imitate those
who through faith and **patience** inherit what has been promised.

HEBREWS 6:12

WELCOME

Maybe you were one of those students back in high school who enjoyed chemistry class. You looked forward to mixing chemicals together in a beaker, heating up the mixture with a Bunsen burner, and logging the results of your "experiment" in a notebook. However, if your teacher was like most, he or she probably warned that if you wanted to get the best results (and the best grade), you needed to take your time with the process and not skip any steps. Otherwise, your impatience would lead to wrong findings . . . and a few chemical explosions.

Patience is critical in our spiritual lives as well. Yet, sadly, it is a virtue that tends to be in short supply in our culture. In today's fast-paced world, we have been conditioned to expect we can get anything we want almost instantaneously. We order everything from shoes to shampoo with the single click of a button. We text, snap, tweet, and get instant "likes" from our online friends. We access news and information around the clock. We are programmed to check our phones every time we hear the "ping" indicating a new message has arrived.

God doesn't operate according to human timing and technology. Rather, he asks you to trust him and *wait* rather than attempt to control the situation in the way you want. It can be difficult to exercise such patience—especially when you can't see the big picture of his plan. But you can always trust that God's ways are "higher than your ways" (Isaiah 55:9) and that he is at work behind the scenes. Our modern world might be moving faster now than at any time in history, but that doesn't change the fact God desires for you to develop patience and self-control.

SHARE

Begin your group time by inviting anyone to share his or her insights from last week's personal study. Next, to kick things off for the group time, discuss the following questions:

✈ When is it the most difficult for you to exercise patience? How do you typically respond when you are forced to wait?

✈ When are some times that you felt God called you to exhibit patience? What happened as a result?

READ

Invite someone to read aloud the following passage. Listen for fresh insights as you hear the verses being read, and then discuss the questions that follow.

> So now, since we have been made right in God's sight by faith in his promises, we can have real peace with him because of what Jesus Christ our Lord has done for us. For because of our faith, he has brought us into this place of highest privilege where we now stand, and we confidently and joyfully look forward to actually becoming all that God has had in mind for us to be.
>
> We can rejoice, too, when we run into problems and trials, for we know that they are good for us—they help us learn to be patient. And patience develops strength of character in us and helps us trust God more each time we use it until finally our hope and faith are strong and steady. Then, when that happens, we are able to hold our heads high no matter what happens and know that all is well, for we know how dearly God loves us, and we feel this warm love everywhere within us because God has given us the Holy Spirit to fill our hearts with his love (Romans 5:1–5 TLB).

What is one key insight that stands out to you from this passage?

What does Paul say are the benefits of developing greater patience in our lives?

WATCH

Play the video segment for session 5. As you watch, use the following outline to record any thoughts that stand out to you.

Notes

We tend to believe God should instantly fix problems when they arise, but the reality is that God uses times of waiting to help us grow and learn to trust in him.

Three powerful quotes about how God uses patience in our lives:

Mark Batterson

John Ortberg

John Piper

Three reasons why patience is powerful in our spiritual lives:

#1: God works in our lives when we follow him

We can't trust our emotions and our feelings to guide us

Patience is a spiritual muscle worth training

#2: God works in our lives when we are waiting on him

There are waiting seasons in our lives

We need to avoid looking for shortcuts

#3: God works even in the interruptions

Almost all of Jesus' ministry occurred as a result of various interruptions

Our patience reveals the glory of God to the world

Four practical ways you can walk in greater patience this week:

    #1: Practice active waiting

    #2: Give yourself ten extra minutes to get to work

    #3: Bite your tongue and pause before you respond

    #4: Put your work down thirty minutes earlier

DISCUSS

Take a few minutes with your group members to discuss what you just watched and explore these concepts in Scripture.

1. Read Isaiah 40:30–31. What does it mean to "wait on the LORD" (NKJV)? What does God promise to those who wait on his timing and trust in him for their needs?

2. What are some ways you are seeking to "ruthlessly eliminate hurry" from your life? What are the benefits of living at more of an unrushed pace?

3. When are times you have been tempted to "follow your heart" instead of waiting for direction from God? What are you currently waiting for God to do in your life?

4. As you look back on your life, how can you see that God was working on your behalf during times of waiting? What might have happened if you had rushed God's plans?

5. Read Luke 5:17–26. How was Jesus interrupted in this story? How did he turn the interruption into an opportunity to minister and instruct the people?

6. How are you pursuing *truth plus patience* in your life? Which of the ideas mentioned in the teaching for growing in patience especially resonated with you? Why?

RESPOND

Briefly review the outline for the video teaching and any notes you took. In the space below, write down the most significant point you took away from this session.

PRAY

Go around the group and let everyone share a request that is requiring them to wait—on another person, on results, on a decision, or on God's answer and his timing. Spend some time in prayer together over these requests, asking God to give each person the power to exercise the discipline required for self-control. Write down these and any other specific requests in the space below so you can remember to continue praying throughout the week.

BETWEEN-SESSIONS PERSONAL STUDY

As the apostle Paul states in 1 Corinthians 13:4, practicing patience and self-control are ways to show your love to others. In fact, they can help you walk in the other fruit of the Spirit—choosing a gentle response over anger, joy instead of irritation, and peace instead of anxiety. As you begin this week's study, you might want to finish reading chapter 7 in *Truth Plus Love* on the benefits of patience and self-control. Record your responses and reflections on your study and consider sharing your observations with the group at the beginning of the next session.

GOD'S TRUTH

In a culture that encourages you to follow your own truth and do whatever it takes to be happy, it may seem old-fashioned and out-dated to wait on God. But the Bible's timeless wisdom is clear that you need to trust your Creator to know what is truly best for you instead of trusting in your feelings, passions, or desires . . . which can often change like the weather.

In Ephesians 6:10–17, Paul urged his readers to defend themselves from the enemy's attacks by putting on spiritual "armor" and covering their hearts with the "breastplate of righteousness." You activate this spiritual defense system when you choose to "guard your heart above all else" (Proverbs 4:23 NLT)—obeying God's Word, following the example of Christ, and walking righteously by faith. You crucify the desires of your flesh, turning away from ungodliness and all "sinful desires, which wage war against your soul" (1 Peter 2:11).

When we give in to sinful desires, we struggle to see God's goodness and resist his truth. Like Adam and Eve in the Garden of Eden, we accept the temptation to think that *we* know what we can and cannot do . . . not God. However, when we choose to follow God, we experience the fullness and freedom of the life he provides. Saved by grace through faith in Jesus' finished work on the cross, we follow in our Savior's footsteps and walk in patient self-control instead of our own sinful passions. As Paul explains this exchange:

> For the grace of God has appeared, bringing salvation for all people, training us to renounce ungodliness and worldly passions, and to live self-controlled, upright, and godly lives in the present age, waiting for our blessed hope, the appearing of the glory of our great God and Savior Jesus Christ, who gave himself for us to redeem us from all lawlessness and to purify for himself a people for his own possession who are zealous for good works (Titus 2:11–14 ESV).

What does it mean to "guard your heart" (Proverbs 4:23)? Why is defending yourself with spiritual armor important to your spiritual growth?

What happens when you *don't* protect yourself with Christ's righteousness and rely on your own judgment?

✱ According to passages cited above, how do you crucify the desires of the flesh and resist ungodliness? How does Christ's example empower you to surrender your own desires?

✱ Where do you see examples of "worldly passions" in our culture? Do you believe it's more difficult to be a Christian today than it was for past generations? Why or why not?

✱ What does it look like to be "zealous for good works"?

✱ How do sin and selfishness hinder a person's enthusiasm for obeying God?

✳ How do patience and self-control contribute to one's ability to follow Jesus and do good works?

PLUS LOVE

Patience and self-control are like muscles that require exercise to grow stronger. Each time you face a major decision and wait on God instead of jumping ahead, it becomes easier at the next crossroads to slow down and put him first. Every time you refrain from doing something you know will harm your relationship with God, you grow stronger to resist temptation the next time. Practicing these spiritual disciplines sets you up for growth and maturity—and enables you to battle against attacks from the *world*, the *flesh*, and the *devil*.

The World

Our culture influences us to be individuals who follow the desires of our hearts, chasing whatever we think will make us happy and pulling us away from godliness, patience, and self-control. Jesus explained the clash between the world and his followers this way: "If the world hates you, keep in mind that it hated me first. If you belonged to the world, it would love you as its own. As it is, you do not belong to the world, but I have chosen you out of the world. That is why the world hates you" (John 15:18–19). Culture's negative influence forces you to choose who to follow: the world or the Word.

🕊 How often do you feel the pull of the world in your daily life? What are some of the ways culture can draw you away from following Jesus?

🕊 What are some ways online offerings and social media conflict with your commitment to balance God's truth with his love? How do you handle these battles when they arise?

The Flesh

Our own sinful desires often pull us away from God. Like spoiled toddlers, we want what we want when we want it! Three areas in which we struggle the most include "the lust of the flesh, the lust of the eyes, and the pride of life" (1 John 2:16). Lust leads to pursuing sexual pleasure outside of God's standards. Covetousness leads us to desiring what other people have and comparing ourselves to them. Pride inflates our sense of importance and results in entitlement.

★ Which of these three—lust, covetousness, or pride—tends to give you the biggest struggle? How have you battled it in the past? How does this fleshly battle hinder your spiritual growth and cause an imbalance in your life?

★ How can you defend yourself against struggles in these three areas? What are some ways you can set yourself up for success?

★ What action can you take right away to help you claim the victory Christ has already won for you?

The Devil

Our spiritual struggles often signal an attack from the enemy. Satan doesn't want us to gain ground for God's kingdom or experience the peace, joy, and contentment we can know when we follow Christ. He tries to get us to doubt God's goodness and trustworthiness.

When have you recently experienced an attack from the enemy that caused you to doubt God's love for you? How did you realize the devil was behind this struggle?

How often do you pray for God's protection against the enemy's attacks? In addition to prayer, what other ways can you defend your heart from the snares of the devil?

EQUALS INFLUENCE

As you consider ways to practice patience and exhibit self-control, look over your online habits. Use the following questions to aid in your assessment and any action plans you develop.

✱ How often do you shop online? What is the ratio between the amount of time you spend browsing and surfing versus actually purchasing something you truly need?

✱ How often do you purchase something on impulse? Do you typically regret these expenditures or just accept it's "what you do"? What are some ways you can safeguard against buying things online that you neither need nor truly want?

✱ Look over your social media accounts and the ones you visit regularly. Would those who don't know you see you're a follower of Jesus? Would they see you as the kind of believer they would want to talk to and enjoy knowing? Why or why not?

✈ How would you describe the tone and personality that comes through your profiles, status pics, comments, and re-tweets? Do they reflect your desire to be more like Christ, or do they look like everyone else's in the world? Explain.

RECOMMENDED READING

In preparation for session 6, read chapters 8–9 in *Truth Plus Love*. Use the space below to note any key points or questions you want to share at the beginning of your next group meeting.

TRUTH PLUS LOVE

For God so **loved** the world that he gave his one and only Son, that whoever believes in him shall not perish but have eternal life.

JOHN 3:16

Speaking **the truth in love**, we will grow to become in every respect the mature body of him who is the head, that is, Christ.

EPHESIANS 4:15

WELCOME

At first glance, a painting seems simple enough . . . just a few splashes of color here and there to form an object or evoke an emotion. But when you actually pick up a brush and try to create one of these works of art, you quickly learn there are a host of other factors to consider—techniques to grasp such as tone, texture, and perspective, to name just a few. You find that art is more than just coloring in between the lines. Rather, the true beauty in a work comes out when artists rely on both the *techniques* they have learned and their own *creativity*.

In many ways, we can "picture" our lives in Christ the same way. We need to have the *truth* of God's Word (the "techniques") so we know his commands, understand how he wants us to lead our lives, and avoid falling into error. As Paul writes, "All Scripture is God-breathed and is useful for teaching, rebuking, correcting and training in righteousness" (2 Timothy 3:16). The *truth* of the gospel is powerful and can change lives.

But we also need to recognize the *love* that God has extended to us (the "creativity") so we can accept it in our hearts, know that we are forgiven, and in turn are able to extend that same love of God to others. As John instructs, "Beloved, let us love one another, for love is from God, and whoever loves has been born of God and knows God" (1 John 4:7 ESV). The *love* of God we experience through the gospel is also powerful and can change lives.

When we exhibit *truth plus love*, we gain the power to influence people in our world for Christ. We create a picture of the Christian life that is beautiful and that others want to have.

SHARE

Begin your group time by inviting anyone to share his or her insights from last week's personal study. Next, to kick things off for the group time, discuss the following questions:

✈ How have you seen the *truth* of the gospel change people's lives? How have you seen the *love* of God transform people's lives?

✈ What has surprised you the most about your experience doing this study? How has your time in the group helped you balance *truth plus love*?

READ

Invite someone to read aloud the following passage. Listen for fresh insights as you hear the verses being read, and then discuss the questions that follow.

There was a man who had two sons. The younger one said to his father, "Father, give me my share of the estate." So he divided his property between them.

Not long after that, the younger son got together all he had, set off for a distant country and there squandered his wealth in wild living. After he had spent everything, there was a severe famine in that whole country, and he began to be in need. So he went and hired himself out to a citizen of that country, who sent him to his fields to feed pigs. He longed to fill his stomach with the pods that the pigs were eating, but no one gave him anything.

When he came to his senses, he said, "How many of my father's hired servants have food to spare, and here I am starving to death! I will set out and go back to my father and say to him: Father, I have sinned against heaven and against you. I am no longer worthy to be called your son; make me like one of your hired servants." So he got up and went to his father.

But while he was still a long way off, his father saw him and was filled with compassion for him; he ran to his son, threw his arms around him and kissed him.

The son said to him, "Father, I have sinned against heaven and against you. I am no longer worthy to be called your son."

But the father said to his servants, "Quick! Bring the best robe and put it on him. Put a ring on his finger and sandals on his feet. Bring the fattened calf and kill it. Let's have a feast and celebrate. For this son of mine was dead and is alive again; he was lost and is found." So they began to celebrate (Luke 15:11–24).

What are some of the *truths* the younger son had to face as a result of his rebellion?

What are some of the ways the father extended *love* to his son when he returned home?

WATCH

Play the video segment for session 6. As you watch, use the following outline to record any thoughts that stand out to you.

Notes

Just as there are fundamental *human* truths that don't change based on our feelings, there are fundamental *spiritual* truths in God's Word that don't change . . . whether we like them or not.

In the second half of Ephesians, Paul gives his readers some forty comands of things God has called them to do—truths to assimilate in their lives and ways to change for the better.

We are called to both *truth plus love*, but often we get that formula wrong:

Love – Truth = Error

Truth – Love = Noise

Our faith is built on the history of the believers before us who influenced the world by walking in *truth plus love* . . . and we will likewise influence those who follow after us.

Two steps that we can take to grow in our love for others:

> *#1:* Experience God's love more deeply in our lives

> *#2:* Share God's love with the world

Our world is starving for joy, peace, gentleness, faithfulness, patience . . . and love. As we walk in these things, it will draw others to our faith in Christ.

A few practical ways you can grow in love this week:

#1: Meditate on God's love for you

#2: Tell your family how much you love them

#3: Forgive the person you need to forgive

#4: T.H.I.N.K. before you speak

#5: Pray for God to give you his love for the world

DISCUSS

Take a few minutes with your group members to discuss what you just watched and explore these concepts in Scripture.

1. Read John 18:33–38. How did Jesus explain his purpose for coming into the world? What does Pilate's response tell you about the way the world views truth?

2. Read Romans 5:8. How does understanding all God did for you *while you were still a sinner*—the peace, gentleness, faithfulness, and patience he gave to you—help you follow his commands to exhibit those same traits in your life?

3. When is a time that walking in God's truth made you unpopular with others? What helped you to remain true to your convictions in spite of the criticism?

4. Consider some of the people before you who have served to influence your faith. How do you want to influence the future generations for Christ?

5. Read Ephesians 3:16–19 and 5:1–2. What was Paul's prayer for his readers? How did Paul want them to live out this love in the way they interacted with others?

6. Which of the ideas mentioned in the teaching for growing this week in *truth plus love* especially resonated with you? Which will you act on this week?

RESPOND

Briefly review the outline for the video teaching and any notes you took. In the space below, write down the most significant point you took away from this session.

PRAY

For this final group meeting, ask God's blessing on each of your lives as you practice balancing his truth with his love. Give thanks for all you have learned together and for all that God has done during your time together in this study. Write down any specific requests in the space below so you can remember to continue praying throughout the week.

FINAL PERSONAL STUDY

As you conclude this study, remember Paul's words in Galatians 5:22–23: "The fruit of the Spirit is love, joy, peace, forbearance, kindness, goodness, faithfulness, gentleness and self-control." As you walk in *truth plus love*, God will continue to develop each of these traits in your life. For this final week, you might want to finish reading chapters 8–9 in *Truth Plus Love* if you have been going through the book as you do the study. Ask the Holy Spirit to help you see where you need to continue focusing your efforts so you can live in the fullness of both God's truth and his love even as you become more effective reflecting both to those around you. Use the questions below to guide your reflection time, and share with your group leader or group members in the upcoming weeks any key points or insights that stood out to you.

GOD'S TRUTH

The author of Hebrews writes, "The word of God is alive and active. Sharper than any double-edged sword, it penetrates even to dividing soul and spirit, joints and marrow; it judges the thoughts and attitudes of the heart" (Hebrews 4:12). The truth of God's Word cuts through the callousness of our hearts and its layers of deception. Although the author refers to it as a sword, it's more like a scalpel that God uses for spiritual surgery on our hearts.

Once we've accepted Christ and are walking in his truth, we no longer follow our own desires or those of the world. We recognize Jesus has won the victory over sin and we are free to enjoy real love, lasting joy, complete peace, and spiritual wholeness. We desire to please our heavenly Father and serve him as we live in the newness of life brought through our salvation. We recognize following

Christ does not limit our ability to enjoy life and its many blessings—in fact, just the opposite! As Jesus promised, "If you hold to my teaching, you are really my disciples. Then you will know the truth, and the truth will set you free" (John 8:31–32).

As we live in God's truth, we know that when we do fall short of God's standard, "If we confess our sins, he is faithful and just and will forgive us our sins and purify us from all unrighteousness" (1 John 1:9). This is the truth of God's Word—that God loves us so much that he sent his Son, Jesus, to be our advocate and atoning sacrifice for our sins (see 2:1). No longer can the enemy pull us away from knowing God's truth and experiencing his love. We experience the freedom ourselves that comes from living in *truth plus love*!

🏹 On a scale of 1 to 10, with 1 being "somewhat doubtful" and 10 being "unwavering belief," how would you rate your faith in the Bible as the absolute source of God's timeless truth? Why did you give yourself this score?

🏹 In what ways has the Bible served to be a "doubled-edged sword" or scalpel that God has used to remove sinful behaviors and shape you into the person he wants you to be?

How should the truth of God's Word motivate your choices and your actions?

How has God's truth brought real and lasting freedom into your life? Explain.

How would you explain the truth of the gospel to someone you know fairly well who has never read the Bible? What verses or passages would you want to use? Why?

PLUS LOVE

Spend a few minutes going back through your notes, answers, and responses from the previous between-sessions studies. Circle or highlight anything that really jumps out or consistently emerges from what you've written. With these in mind, consider the following questions.

✈ How have you grown the most since you started this study? What has contributed to this progress and improvement?

✈ What did you enjoy most about the time you spent with your group members? How did God use the experience to enhance your understanding of *truth plus love*?

✈ What do you know now about balancing truth and love that you didn't grasp before you started this study? How will this new insight affect the way you relate to other people?

🗡 At the beginning of this study, you were asked to conduct a personal inventory of the spiritual fruit in your life. Take this assessment again, writing down a number below between *1* and *5*, with 1 indicating "absent in my life / needs work" and 5 indicating "abundant in my life / overflowing."

___ Love	___ Joy	___ Peace
___ Patience	___ Kindness	___ Goodness
___ Faithfulness	___ Gentleness	___ Self-Control

Compare these responses with the ones you noted in session 1, and then say a prayer of thankfulness to God for the growth that has taken place in your life.

EQUALS INFLUENCE

In the coming weeks, contact someone from your group and plan a time to meet together. Listen carefully as the other person shares what he or she has learned and how he or she has grown. Ask how you can encourage the person to continue growing in his or her faith . . . perhaps choosing one or two of the fruits of the Spirit as your primary focus. Commit to praying for each other as you continue living in the fullness of God's truth and the freedom of his love.

As you keep all that you've learned and experienced in mind, think about what God is calling you to do next to have the greatest impact for his kingdom. Then . . . don't wait! Let God use you to show others the impact that *truth plus love* can have on their lives!

LEADER'S GUIDE

Thank you for your willingness to lead your group through this study! What you have chosen to do is valuable and will make a great difference in the lives of others. The rewards of being a leader are different from those of participating, and we hope that as you lead you will find your own walk with Jesus deepened by this experience.

Truth Plus Love is a six-session study built around video content and small-group interaction. As the group leader, just think of yourself as the host of a dinner party. Your job is to take care of your guests by managing all the behind-the-scenes details so that when everyone arrives, they can just enjoy time together.

As the group leader, your role is not to answer all the questions or reteach the content—the video, book, and study guide will do most of that work. Your job is to guide the experience and cultivate your small group into a kind of teaching community. This will make it a place for members to process, question, and reflect—not receive more instruction.

Before your first meeting, make sure everyone in the group gets a copy of the study guide. This will keep everyone on the same page and help the process run more smoothly. If some group members are unable to purchase the guide, arrange it so that people can share the resource with other group members. Giving everyone access to all the material will position this study to be as rewarding an experience as possible. Everyone should feel free to write in his or her study guide and bring it to group every week.

SETTING UP THE GROUP

You will need to determine with your group how long you want to meet each week so you can plan your time accordingly. Generally, most groups like to meet for either ninety minutes or two hours, so you could use one of the following schedules:

Section	90 Minutes	120 Minutes
WELCOME (members arrive and get settled)	5 minutes	15 minutes
SHARE (discuss one or more of the opening questions for the session)	10 minutes	15 minutes
READ (discuss the questions based on the Scripture reading for the week)	10 minutes	15 minutes
WATCH (watch the teaching material together and take notes)	30 minutes	20 minutes
DISCUSS (discuss the Bible study questions you selected ahead of time)	30 minutes	40 minutes
RESPOND / PRAY (complete the individual closing exercise, pray together as a group, and dismiss)	5 minutes	15 minutes

As the group leader, you will want to create an environment that encourages sharing and learning. A church sanctuary or formal classroom may not be as ideal as a living room, because those locations can feel formal and less intimate. No matter what setting you choose, provide enough comfortable seating for everyone, and, if possible, arrange the seats in a semicircle so everyone can see the video easily. This will make transition between the video and group conversation more efficient and natural.

Also, try to get to the meeting site early so you can greet participants as they arrive. Simple refreshments create a welcoming atmosphere and can be a wonderful addition to a group study evening. Try to take food and pet allergies into account to make your guests as comfortable as possible. You may also want to consider offering childcare to couples with children who want to attend. Finally, be sure your media technology is working properly. Managing these details up front will make the rest of your group experience flow smoothly and provide a welcoming space in which to engage the content of *Truth Plus Love*.

STARTING THE GROUP TIME

Once everyone has arrived, it's time to begin the group. Here are some simple tips to make your group time healthy, enjoyable, and effective.

First, begin the meeting with a short prayer and remind the group members to put their phones on silent. This is a way to make sure you can all be present with one another and with God. Next, give each person a few minutes to respond to the questions in the "Share" and "Read" sections. This won't require as much time in session 1, but beginning in session 2, people will need more time to share their insights from their personal studies. Usually, you won't answer the discussion questions yourself, but you should go first with the "Share" and "Read" questions, answering briefly and with a reasonable amount of transparency.

At the end of session 1, invite the group members to complete the between-sessions personal studies for that week. Explain that you will be providing some time before the video teaching next week for anyone to share insights. Let them know sharing is optional, and it's no problem if they can't get to some of the between-sessions activities some weeks. It will still be beneficial for them to hear from the other participants and learn about what they discovered.

LEADING THE DISCUSSION TIME

Now that the group is engaged, it's time to watch the video and respond with some directed small-group discussion. Encourage all the group members to participate in the discussion, but make sure they know they don't have to do so. As the discussion progresses, you may want to follow up with comments such as, "Tell me more about that," or, "Why did you answer that way?" This will allow the group participants to deepen their reflections and invite meaningful sharing in a nonthreatening way.

Note that you have been given multiple questions to use in each session, and you do not have to use them all or even follow them in order. Feel free to pick and choose questions based on either the needs of your group or how the conversation is flowing. Also, don't be afraid of silence. Offering a question and allowing up to thirty seconds of silence is okay. It allows people space to think about how they want to respond and also gives them time to do so.

As group leader, you are the boundary keeper for your group. Do not let anyone (yourself included) dominate the group time. Keep an eye out for group members who might be tempted to "attack" folks they disagree with or try to "fix" those having struggles. These kinds of behaviors can derail a group's momentum, so they need to be steered in a different direction. Model active listening and encourage everyone in your group to do the same. This will make your group time a safe space and create a positive community.

The group discussion leads to a closing time of individual reflection and prayer. Encourage the participants to take a few moments to review what they've learned during the session and write down their thoughts to the "Respond" section. This will help them cement the big ideas in their minds as you close the session. Conclude by having the participants break into smaller groups of two to three people to pray for one another.

Thank you again for taking the time to lead your group. You are making a difference in the lives of others and having an impact on the kingdom of God!